"In *Four Reincarnations*, Max Ritvo brings us along where poetry needs to go; away from the small confessional and into a big world of death, love, and metaphysics. While allowing for the possibility of a confessional mode in the details, Ritvo's poems take stock of the nineteenth-century sublime, adding the contemporary death of God, and going forward with bravery, irony, and the most compassionate sense of humor. The relationship he hews between language and the body is both original and hard won. His lyric complicity is between self, dedicatee, reader, and world. Ritvo's ear for language is beautiful, as is his spirit. His poems defy solipsism and enter a cosmology of unconditional love. How lucky I am that I found Max Ritvo and his poetry; he makes me love poetry again."

—SARAH RUHL

"This is poetry written in the dark light of dying young. You feel the truth of this poetry too deeply to want to talk about it in your own words. You want to give it to other people still back here in health, to say to them, 'Here: the earthly gift of this poet of genius, Max Ritvo.' To Ritvo himself, we might say what he says to his wife in one of these poems: 'Thou art me before I am myself.' In the sense not of death, but of most ardent life."

—JEAN VALENTINE

"If you could confect a numinous cauldron and stir into it the lumens of Christopher Smart's Spiritual Musick, the spirit-hounds of Hopkins's 'terrible crystals,' the hysteria of Monty Python's antics, the grace and depth of Keats's early wisdoms, you would render incarnate the first and final book of Max Ritvo's, *Four Reincarnations*. The poems flicker like fireflies let loose from their captivity in a mason jar, fulgurating like Nobodaddy's business. Somehow, somewhere, Ritvo must have begun as an infant scholar, a prodigy, a young man of the rarest and most prescient gifts. This is a dazzling collection, rife with life, and with death, impending. This book, then, will be the afterlife. Ritvo's work is extracelestial, riddled with brilliance and with ecstasies. We are lucky to have this luminous collection in our world. It will go on. And then on."

—LUCIE BROCK-BROIDO

"Armed with intelligence, valor, audacity, and grace, Max Ritvo's imagination pushes back against one grim reality after another in its insistence on celebrating being embodied in the first place. No poet I can think of undertakes the transmutation of suffering into art with anything resembling Ritvo's wild theatricality, inclusiveness, and tonal range. Dizzying, out of proportion, poundingly felt, fantastical, fanatical, urgently constructed, confessional, gaudy, absurd, mystic, harrowing—the fact that Ritvo's work can be described in so many ways is testament to its complexity. The fact that we can never quite describe it in full is evidence of its irreplaceability. The fact that it haunts so many of its readers is proof that it has already become a necessary and sustaining part of us—some measure of our acquired wisdom, some portion of our vision of what it means to be alive."

—TIMOTHY DONNELLY

FOUR

REINCARNATIONS

FOUR
REINCARNATIONS

POEMS

MAX RITVO

MILKWEED EDITIONS

Published 2016 by Milkweed Editions
Printed in the United States of America
Cover design by Mary Austin Speaker
Cover illustration by Autumn Von Plinsky
Author photo by Ashley Woo
17 18 19 20   6 5 4 3
First Edition

Milkweed Editions, an independent nonprofit publisher, gratefully acknowledges sustaining support from the Jerome Foundation; the Lindquist & Vennum Foundation; the McKnight Foundation; the National Endowment for the Arts; the Target Foundation; and other generous contributions from foundations, corporations, and individuals. Also, this activity is made possible by the voters of Minnesota through a Minnesota State Arts Board Operating Support grant, thanks to a legislative appropriation from the arts and cultural heritage fund, and a grant from the Wells Fargo Foundation Minnesota. For a full listing of Milkweed Editions supporters, please visit www.milkweed.org.

Library of Congress Cataloging-in-Publication Data

Names: Ritvo, Max, 1990- author.
Title: Four reincarnations : poems / Max Ritvo.
Description: First edition. | Minneapolis : Milkweed Editions, 2016.
Identifiers: LCCN 2016030740| ISBN 9781571314901 (hardcover) | ISBN 9781571319579 (ebook)
Classification: LCC PS3618.I8 A6 2016 | DDC 811/.6--dc23
LC record available at https://lccn.loc.gov/2016030740

Milkweed Editions is committed to ecological stewardship. We strive to align our book production practices with this principle, and to reduce the impact of our operations in the environment. We are a member of the Green Press Initiative, a nonprofit coalition of publishers, manufacturers, and authors working to protect the world's endangered forests and conserve natural resources. *Four Reincarnations* was printed on acid-free 100% postconsumer-waste paper by Edwards Brothers Malloy.

to my master, to my wife, to my mother,
to my fathers, to my sisters, to my nephew,
to my teachers, to my friends, to my exes,
to my shrinks, and to my doctors

Contents

1

2

1

LIVING IT UP

The bed is on fire, and are you laughing?

You leave the bed
and leave me without thought.

The springs want to embrace each other
but they're afraid if they break

their spiral, they will never
be able to hold anyone.

I wish you would let me know
how difficult it is to love me.

Then I would know you love me
beneath all that difficulty.

You are tending not only to me, you tell me,
but to your other child—the air,

and air puts his feet in my slippers,
and air scrubs his teeth on my brush,

and we must learn to share a bed,
we must learn to share a body.

The money is running out.
We will have to split one needle

this winter—one end for me,
one end for air.

THE CURVE

Something, call it X, wanted a body
so it made our bodies.
But our bodies weren't right for it—

gum around the bones,
a rash of gold or black,

eyes like blisters
leaking fondness.

*

X realized all animal bodies were like this, so it made language.

*

Language forced X into the body
like carbonation into a soda.

When I hear the word *rock*,
a translucent lump
shimmers in front of the world.

To its right, a piece of glass cuts a clear finger,
and to its left, there pulses a rocky, low, cold crust.

*

Though the images
vary exhaustingly and troublingly,
I always remember
the spoke of earth
cutting into the ocean
we saw from above, on a bicycle ride,

the sheen of the bicycles
spreading over the earth,
distinct from the ocean's sheen.
The sheens alarmingly similar to one another
to be so close together—like two bodies making love.

*

We imagine a vertical meadow
complicated into our world *needlessly*
but complication is all X ever wanted for us.
We misunderstand purity. This is purity.

*

I am your lover and X's.
I am too good a lover
to ever be bored:

Skinny, hairy-chested,
made of pellets of rice,
cheeping in a way that's
endearing and inappropriate,
confused, surprised at the confusion,
surprised at the surprise,
and so on, very tiringly, so on.

THE SENSES

Everything feels so good to me:
my wool hat,
the cocoon of dryness in my throat.

The sound of burning vegetables
is like a quiet, clean man folding sheets.

But I keep having thoughts—
this thought always holding at bay the next thought
until it sours into yet

another picture of dissatisfaction
that loves to be thought,

another pear, ugly
as the head
of a man who is thinking.

I thought my next thought would be a vision of my suffering;
I thought I would understand the yellow lightning in a painted storm—
the crucial way it disappears
when I imagine myself flung
headlong into the painting.

Instead I have this picture of dissatisfaction,
the thought not rising, but splitting in half
on the unanswered question of lightning,

my mind
like a black glove
you mistake for a man
in the middle of a blizzard.

HOLDING A FRESHWATER FISH IN A PAIL
ABOVE THE SEA

He strips health out
of the water,
reminding me
of my mother.

I walk in sea
and hold my sweet
fish above me,
no small feat

given the rice-
hard salt scraping
my eyeballs twice
each blink of lid.

I put the pail
in the ocean
and then unveil
the decorous

frail, white-eyed koi.
But the salt, I
think, will destroy
his rocking breath.

Where he wants space
he will get salt.
Where key traces
of the silence

should hang inside
his cathedral
of musical
blood—

Instead, delicious
crystal drills
will crack it all
open; the church,

its ebbs and flows.
I scoop the fish
up by its nose,   *edible?*
a forked affair.

I show you him.
Looks fine to me
you say (Ha!), dim
and lovely you.

This happens more
times, stopping and
starting, me showing
you my full hand,

my fish. Where have
you gone? I was
hoping to wake
from this dream

with you drawing
the curtains, a gold

glow on the sheet
wrapping me up.

You aren't here
but I'm aware
that somewhere
you have moved.

THE WATERCOLOR EULOGY
for Melissa Carroll

When you leave my mind,
the last piece of you to leave
is your hands.

When you go to the earth
the last part of you visible
above what is either sand or clay
isn't a hand, but a glowing shroud.

The black goose
with your name in its throat
and my name in its stomach
will cough you up with her hoots:
part jelly, part watch,
part bone, part me,
part power.

There is a dead language buried in English.
There is a word no one remembers
for a temple
with a bowl of millet sealed
in each brick.
When you are buried, the word
will grow a *ssa* sound.
Its meaning will change
to specify you as the builder.

No one can speak the language you will rewrite.

I know this isn't the heaven we wanted.
What ever is?

And soon I'll join you
amid the terms
for tiny bottles of defunct potions
and no longer understood passions
and together we'll bury
our own particular *I love you.*

I wouldn't mind its being sealed off with us, in our brick of earth.

HI, MELISSA

I have spoken to you of heaven—
I simply meant the eyes are suns that see.
Seeing is the faces' nervous delicious Lord.

Listening to you makes me naked.
When I kiss your ankle I am silencing an oracle.
The oracle speaks from the hill of your ankle.

POEM TO MY LITTER

My genes are in mice, and not in the banal way
that Man's old genes are in the Beasts.

My doctors split my tumors up and scattered them
into the bones of twelve mice. We give

the mice poisons I might, in the future, want
for myself. We watch each mouse like a crystal ball.

I wish it was perfect, but sometimes the death we see
doesn't happen when we try it again in my body.

My tumors are old, older than mice can be.
They first grew in my flank a decade ago.

Then they went to my lungs, and down my femurs,
and into the hives in my throat that hatch white cells.

The mice only have a tumor each, in the leg.
Their tumors have never grown up. Uprooted

and moved. Learned to sleep in any bed
the vast body turns down. Before the tumors can spread

they bust open the legs of the mice. Who bleed to death.
Next time the doctors plan to cut off the legs

in the nick of time so the tumors will spread.
But I still have both my legs. To complicate things further,

mouse bodies fight off my tumors. We have to give
the mice AIDS so they'll harbor my genes peacefully.

I want my mice to be just like me. I don't have any children.
I named them all Max. First they were Max 1, Max 2,

but now they're all just Max. No playing favorites.
They don't know they're named, of course.

They're like children you've traumatized
and tortured so they won't let you visit.

I hope, Maxes, some good in you is of me.
Even my suffering is good, in part. Sure I swell

with rage, fear—the stuff that makes you see your tail
as a bar on the cage. But then the feelings pass.

And since I do absolutely nothing (my pride, like my fur,
all gone) nothing happens to me. And if a whole lot

of nothing happens to you, Maxes, that's peace.
Which is what we want. Trust me.

Leor

DAWN OF MAN

After the cocoon I was in a human body
instead of a butterfly's. All along my back

there was great pain—I groped to my feet
where I felt wings behind me, trying

to tilt me back. They succeeded in doing so
after a day of exertion. I called that time,

overwhelmed with the ghosts of my wings, sleep.
My thoughts remained those of a caterpillar—

I took pleasure in climbing trees. I snuck food
into all my pains. My mouth produced language

which I attempted to spin over myself
and rip through happier and healthier.

I'd do this every few minutes. I'd think to myself
What made me such a failure?

It's all a little touchingly pathetic. To live like this,
a grown creature telling ghost stories,

staring at pictures, paralyzed for hours.
And even over dinner or in bed—

still hearing the stories, seeing the pictures—
an undertow sucking me back into myself.

I'm told to set myself goals. But my mind
doesn't work that way. I, instead, have wishes

for myself. Wishes aren't afraid
to take on their own color and life—

like a boy who takes a razor from a high cabinet,
puffs out his cheeks, and strips them bloody.

BLACK BULLS

My mind is
three black bulls on
three hills of sand, far apart.

My loved ones
sleep in clay hollows.

If I turn from you, you will go back
to your clay hollow.

The aqueducts of the city of my language
clot with lather.

The world is bad
and I am bad.

Three black bulls on three hills
of sand are stretching apart
the sheet of my language, crawling with ants.

This is the basis
upon which we seek company:
I am bad,
the world is bad.

Three black bulls stomp the hills of sand
into blistered glass.

Their hooves swelter against these
wrong bells.

I am so sorry that you have come to this mind of mine.

2

FOR CROW

We tended to a crow,
and now it's fine.
It shakes its head, and eats crickets,
forgetful bird
that you put in a pouch to make sleep.

They said his eyes were blue because he was young.
Black blurs the eyes of crows as they grow old—
all motion
disruption in a lake of light.

I am a crow, and
I think you are mostly a pattern of motion
and I am a leaf—and your hands fan under
and over me, and create a little space
in which the thing in my life that adds up
is my motion.

I think you can be traced
most easily by the echoes of your kinetics, my love.
Your lips, neck, arms,
these are not a harbor;
the you-around-you is the harbor.

In our bed, in the dark,
it is not sound, not outline,
but the motion of you
that brings to the surface of my body
all of the apparentness
of a settling glass of muddy water.

How I feel is then forgotten,
and instead I find myself
moving, joy, moving!

TO RANDAL, CROW-STEALER,
LORD OF THE GREENHOUSE

I master the technology to make bricks.
I build altars clumped with fire.
I am not afraid to light
a flower and destroy her beauty;
the crispy flower has been taken to a godly feast.

Do you pity my imagination? It will kill you.
My mother will kill you.
She is my imagination.

I am a leather horse, and my mother is riding me.
You are a man: alert, passionate.
You sit in an almond of glossy hair.
You are capable of being persuaded by fine argument.
You even smile eagerly when convinced.

Remember what a great time we had in the first stanza?
And now this: me blubbering to mommy
over your brilliance.
Tell me what it's like to be you. *Well Max,*

imagine if you stayed
by your bricks after your sacrifice
until your body warmed them.

It's called being indoors, and it's a good first step.

I'd die of thirst!

Imagine prying fingers through the bricks,
making tunnels your mind first saw as ghosts.

Imagine pressing your lips to the pipes
and sipping dew from the outside.

You are exquisitely sensitive.
I imagine defecating over your eyebrows: a unibrow.

And what about my godly flower? You still haven't accounted for that!
I inhale the flower's smoke, and it allows me to control every inch of
my body,
and a little man emerges: this is called being possessed.

I dance out here, trouserless on the salt flat, dazzled by hail,
because every gesture perfects my body
into the little man's happy home.

You have no flowers in your indoor dark, fireless Randal!

Max, I have invented glass, through which the sun may light my flowers.

One of these days you'll be stable enough to make a woman happy,
and that will go a long way.

*

The secret to making people happy, Randal,
I call at your departing, shiny suit,
is that I am the people!

SKY-SEX DREAMS OF RANDAL

I am raving at you
with extremely good eye contact.

I fancy, lovely, that there are many drains
to circle.

Look at me and bore me,
bore me good and flaccid.

That's right, now I'm in a getup,
dressed like a palm-tree lady—hula skirt, the whole shebang.

I have reached the end of suffering
and sat on the dark porch:

On the white ledge, a spider throws up the fat
of a bee.
Three white wood chairs in the mud,
a glass-topped table sealed into
a knot of pampas grass.
The chairs watching shadows on the glass top

like white poodles, all named *Handsome*,
from different phases of your life,
watching television pictures of your sex dreams play out.

Sob, elf.
Yelp, gnome, of the end.

STALKING MY EX-GIRLFRIEND IN A PASTURE

In the beginning, the Worldly Winds
portioned us hides of equal thickness.

But then one day my ex's glossy vagina spoke.
The breath came from inside—
a womb-rung bell of molten gold
unfed by the Winds:

You are a cart that I can teach to be two bicycles.

I wetted my hands in her
and her eyebrows and smile made a circuit in her face;
she described an orgasm
so imaginatively that I longed to become her.

She instructed me to unyoke the mind and body
so that the mind could speak
as the body came

but I split wrong. Only my mind split—
into an array of sirens with
show tunes played in between them.

Or maybe it was only my body
and that is why I am naked and bloody.

I want to dress to the nines—
to wear a navy tuxedo
with a white chrysanthemum in the lapel.

Then I can approach her,
submit her body to the operations
of the gods, expose her
bell to the Winds,
and take back the hide she took

to be the sheet
on my eternal sickbed.

*

I refuse the doctor's fizzy tincture
because each bubble is me
until it pops on my tongue
and then it's you.

MOMMY HARANGUES POOR RANDAL

Money is self-comprehending,
take a hard look in the mirror,

your brow is brutal, your teeth are for meat,
your eyes are globes and hunched beneath them
is *my* ghost who blinks them shut, who pulls out
your tears, I'm finished. We're finished.

Go outside and play, but if you come
knocking on my door when you're done
don't be surprised if I say *Who's there?*

And if you *keep* pushing, and dare
name yourself, here's a warning—
they call it a punch line because I punch you
in the fucking face if you step over the line.

LYRIC COMPLICITY FOR ONE

I wanted to speak with a woman
so passionately and imaginatively that our personalities
would dissolve, we would begin to lie,
and a thing between us
much more beautiful than either of our voices
would begin to speak—a lyric complicity.

Instead, imagine a fisherman
rubbing hot water on his throat.
His mother once said
gargle hot water when your throat's tight.
He can't remember the word *gargle* in the memory,
only his mother fanning out her fingers as she said it,
small, precise, and a little wicked.
So now he gets it wrong, remembering the fingers, feeling forlorn.

Beneath him swim bluefin tuna at fifty miles an hour,
fast and invisible as the wicked fingers.
These sea-seams, these black-bodied cloaks of guts,
are just as dazed as the thoughts of the fisherman.
For every thought, a new fish soars
right under the anchored boat—
a lullaby to quiet another lullaby.

3

POEM ABOUT MY WIFE BEING PERFECT
AND ME BEING AFRAID

You chase my face with your face
by making my faces:

Your lips, right after mine, form a crescent
and wax and wane with all the moons
of my mouth.

You catch up and have my thoughts.
Your brain binds around mine, a gold gauze.

You have my thoughts faster than I can.
The mouth made from our lips
pours chilly water
out the pipe.

We go faster than I imagined \
my mind built time or built itself.

I see behind the documents:
the gauze swelling with gold
blood into a halo.

Thou art me before I am myself.

abandon/desire

WHEN I CRITICIZE YOU, I'M JUST TRYING TO CRITICIZE THE UNIVERSE

Why do you shit so much—is it cancer or anxiety?

I go to the bathroom to visit my ex-girlfriends.

They're two lily pads, fire-white—one in the bath,
the other in the toilet—and they call me Kermit,
and beg Kermit to swim.

My body's voices, normally so quarrelsome,
grow warm and weepy, and start
to sing together "Take Me to the Water."

I thought I might sleep in the bathroom tonight.
Please don't be mad, wife.

I'm not mad at you,
I'm mad at the universe unfolding in your body.

Can't you think of me as a person?

Me seeing the universe in your body
is what makes you such a <u>people person</u>.

*

I went to the bathroom to sleep.
I dreamt two dreams—one inside the other—
The outer dream, a shell,
the deeper dream, a yolk.

a dialogue

36

Next to him, a woman is completely silent.
Feeding him the bean
becomes her only thought,
even when he tries to admire her beauty
or make her laugh.
She folds into the green glow
and nobody will listen to his news.

The sound wasn't a gun.
It was a kiss.
It's my mother—
I have to go.

POEM SET IN THE DAY AND IN THE NIGHT

Just do things that are meaningful to you.
Go to the beach, says the Doc.

The man lies on his stomach.
The sand is fine, chewed through
by the waves many times over.

The sun is wide, like an eye cut open,
and it blasts the man so that his whole shadow
scuttles beneath his belly.

The shadow grows dense
and the man sweats himself thin.

The man becomes a web
and his shadow becomes a spider.

It's not that his life passes to the shadow—
but a tipping happens, as in an hourglass,

and suddenly there's a new order
to the life he never knew was shared.

That night a cricket kills himself in the man.

It's unbearable, his silk body thrilled through
with the screams. All the man is: a speaker—

and not loud enough to communicate
the fear to God.

Enough, however, to bring the spider.

Who brings a kind of relief.

Is it a sin to take the moon? On a night like this?

To bathe the body in soapy light, sipping
gray moisture like beads on a necklace?

But what night isn't like this?

The monster is quiet on his long white limbs—
you only notice what he mops up.

And while there's no such thing as pure silence,
memory breaks apart

and that's close enough.
Close enough for sleep:

A sweet face
rips in half and

you pass through it
like a curtain.

On the other side, you're the body again,
and the shadow is again shadow.

You can enjoy anything—you don't remember
how clumsy the old hands were, how picky the tongue.

When you smile, every tooth is a perfect O,
when you write, every letter is a perfect O,

when you weep, sorrow comes clean out.
Hello again, you say. Hello again.

POEM TO MY DOG, MONDAY, ON NIGHT
I ACCIDENTALLY ATE MEAT

The lights went out on Monday
lying on a green rug—
wanting to make noise, only—

a visitation left
in his small white body.

The symbol is outrageous: like a hungry man
in your soul slamming down jam jars.

Thank God for the past tense, and its order,
and that the dog died before it was symbolic.

Monday, the Hunt left your bed.
It found a white bulb
in your body to sleep in.

Monday, it's leaving me too.
Why does life love flowers most
when they are still bulbs?

—the plant and her roots
all stalks, stalking themselves in a circle
in the dark?

Monday, with your millions of soft horns,
I will slip behind your poodle eyes,
loading myself like a cartridge of light.

I will live in your small ecstatic brain
and take your life,

and you can take mine,
and we won't give our lives to cancer,
but to each other.

And thank God for the future,
where we levitate,
or maybe Oblivion curls down our ears
into wings, or figs that He eats.

TROY

Tooth and tooth
Tooth and tooth
Baboon

There are tents where the sand
is made of lice
under the light of the moon.

Tooth and moon and tooth
Tooth and tooth
Baboon

They come,
they mate; it's ugly.

A circle of apes.
An eight of many brown apes
around the white naked points of the tents.

In the corner of the tent are fine pieces of art, fine things.
A candelabrum melts, or the sand crawls up it.

The racket!
Inside the tents, the howls thud like food.
We need more room in our mouths.
The chef makes Eucharist of the food,
threading his hairs into the meats.
It's his only way.

The watchman in his tall tower
worries:
Every day he must make his yo-yo string
a little tighter.

HEAVEN IS US BEING A FLOWER TOGETHER

Victoria, I think death comes at blindness.

I think pupils are sails
and death is when the wind goes slack.

Winter, by being so white,
is trying to talk to me—

closing communicated to one who sees death
as white worms
riddling the apple of the eye.

You think death comes at the cessation of touch.
You are a flower bulb
that can feel even in winter earth.

The cold is a line that will not bend,
drawn through you foot to head.

Heat is a planet
fleeing its own cold line.

I have written this poem inside of you.
I am clutched in with your mother blood,
feeling your bends in the dark,
becoming a soft bend in your body.

We are becoming a bulb
in the ground of the living,
in the winter of being alive. *Richard III*

AFTERNOON

When I was about to die
my body lit up
like when I leave my house
without my wallet.

What am I missing? I ask,
patting my chest
pocket.

And I am missing everything living
that won't come with me
into this sunny afternoon

—my body lights up for life
like all the wishes being granted in a fountain
at the same instant—
all the coins burning the fountain dry—

and I give my breath
to a small, bird-shaped pipe.

In the distance, behind several voices
haggling, I hear a sound like heads
clicking together. Like a game of pool
played with people by machines.

4

SECOND DREAM

I hold my face
in the bed.

Me: *What is my future?*
Shon: *Flowers. You are marrying flowers.*

PLUSH BUNNY

My poor little future,
you could practically fit in a shoebox
like the one I kept 'pecial bunny in
when I decided I was too old to sleep with her.
I'd put a lid on the box every night.
I knew she couldn't breathe—she was stuffed,
but I thought she'd like the dark, the quiet.
She had eyes, I could see them.
They were two stitches. My future has eyes,
for a while. Then my future has stitches,
like 'pecial's. Then cool cotton, like her guts.
Of course there is another world. But it is not elsewhere.
The eye traps it so where heaven should be
you see shadows. You start to reek.
That's you moving on.

CROW SAYS GOODBYE

There is a white stone cliff
over a dropping slope
sliced along with bare trees.

In the center of the cliff
is a round dry fountain of polished stone.

By seizing my whole body up as I clench my hand
I am able to open the fountain
into a drain, revealing below it the sky,
the trees, a brown and uncertain ground.

This is how my heart works, you see?
This is how love works?
Have some sympathy for the great spasms
with which I must open myself to love
and close again, and open.

And if I leapt into the fountain, there is just no telling:
I might sever myself clean, or crack the gold bloom of my head,
and I don't know what uncertain ground I might fold on like a sack.

APPEAL TO MY FIRST LOVE

You can only swallow when I swallow—
you swallow every time you see me swallow.

The coloring book fills with love, over and over—
you turn each page over, blotting them red.

It's a flipbook as stultifying and repetitive as your heart when it adores me.
It's the most beautiful thing I've ever laid eyes on.
Flipbook of sky in love,
the flipbook of true love.

Come back, this cereal is gross, these cartoons are whiny.

Adore me to sleep before sleep can adore me on its own terms.

THE BIG LOSER

The guardian angel sits in the tree
above the black lip of street
the man walks down.
He calls the man *Cargo*.

The angel sees a pinewood box in place of the man,
and the street he walks is a boat,
the hull like a coal crater.

Somewhere in the real world there is such a boat and box.

The angels call these overlays *dreams*
and believe they crop up because angels
can't sleep but want to—

space falls apart when you have unlimited time.

*

The cargo is rattling in the boat.
Maybe it's just the waves, maybe it's rats.
What's the difference? Either way: it's the box.

The angel sends the man
a happy vision from his past—the time

he fed birthday cake
to his goldfish
after an unsuccessful party.

57

The angel thinks he's applying lemon oil
to the creaky, wounded wood of the box.
He knows it's palliative, but it's beautiful.

*

The man reaches the end of the street. He's a sick man
and he starts to ponder death
as he often does these days:

All of death is *right here*
—the gods, the dark, a moon.
Where was I expecting death
to take me if everywhere it is
is on earth?

At life's close, you're like the child whose parents
step out for a drive—

everyone *else* out on a trip,
but the child remains in the familiar bed,
feeling old lumps like new
in the mattress—the lights off—

not sleeping, for who can sleep
with the promise of a world beyond the door?

*

That night the child dreams
he's inside the box.

It's burning hot, the heat coming
from bugs and worms
raping and devouring one another.

He starts the hard work
of the imagination,
learning to minister to the new dream.

Perhaps all that's needed is a little rain—
for everyone to drink and have a bath.

Outside: a car humming,
somewhere, his mother's singing.

THE VACUUM PLANET OF THE PEE PEE
PRIESTESS

Every day a chicken dies so that my mom may live:
their corpses, a tide; her teeth, beheaded cliffs;
her gums, the rubber blades of heaven.

Deeper in her, vagrants
made of shadow
pack the city of her body.

I'm a little bum in there who says
I'm alone instead of other people.

Panic is a complicated city
fed exclusively on chicken.

Turn on the fan.
Steaming chicken spins it.
Flip the light and a geyser of neck
blood will force open your pupils.

All my shadowy friends are memories from her brain.
I am solid and pink and come from the egg in her stomach.

I was lonely for a pink person
who doesn't think exactly like my mom,
so I headed north

to the place where her brain
moans chilly
and low, like lightning that wants to stay.

I hear my own voice, in the moaning,
from the world beyond:

THE BLIMP

I thought above my head there was a blimp
and it trailed hoses covered in tacks,
some of which inhaled
and some of which blew air.
And I thought the blimp was fate
and the shadow it cast
was fate's decision that I stay
in shadow. And I thought the world
was growing craggy: everywhere illuminated
with white chalk,
but the shadow went down,
down, and I was in a wheelchair
riding down and my body was swelling,
my stomach and limbs
swelling, and I was asked to describe
some letters scratched on the wall
but making sense of them
was difficult, so I loved them, like mother,
and many years later, in the spreading
serenity, there was no place for this
as there is never a place
for struggle in a living room
where someone is pouring you ice water
in exchange for grateful silence you
learn to love.

THE END

The moon was dark
like it had taken too many pills
to produce light.

The earth fell apart
into pockets,
the many things in it
noticing where they were, and surfacing.

Heaven was a vacuum—
the earth, a dirty carpet.

What is there to say?
All the animals went blind:
the pigs out in the countryside,
and my dear dog who used to fetch.

I wondered, at one point,
if I had in fact killed myself—
if death just meant spending
all your time with your past.

The more there is, the more loss there is—
true not only of the world, but of perceiving it,
even of the imagination sizzling on top of it.

I have a dark bruise on my body
where a tail would come.
If I put pure water in my mouth
and cough it out, it's mud.

Enoch has written
We are made in His image
but God may have many images.
He may want even more.

Perhaps He is using my body
to remake His
into a kind of thinking dust.

This is, however, an abnegation
of my choice. I am here,
no voices in my ear,
no madness but the one of life—

TOUCHING THE FLOOR

I touch my palms to the floor
and granite bulls surge up my arms
and lock in my shoulders.
Water flecks on my back
and my head is shaved
by bladed cream.

But then my time in my body is up
and it's time for my mind:
It seeks wisdom
and the bulls fall into a well,
their faces falling apart—

I want to know what their last words are
but their lips are fading into the purple.

I put my hands into the ground again
but bulls come only for the body
and never for the mind.

I used to want infinite time with my thoughts.
Now I'd prefer to give all my time
to a body that's dying from cancer.

*

O Body, playmate of the kiln,
darkener of sky and water,

could you squeeze shut
the little mouths talking my hands out of my body?

ZYPREXA, THE SNOW PILLS

have too many wounds to zip up,
brain becoming a suit of zippers,
soberly shutting.

SNOW ANGELS

We call it snow
when the parts of God, | *myth*

too small to bear, contest our bodies
for the possession of our smallest sensations.

The snow brings suffering to the only thing small enough
to have lived peaceably next to suffering. *A*

THE HANGING GARDENS

A land and its peoples are often spoken of together.
This is a description of just a land
and not its peoples:

A bare tree here is not like
a bare tree elsewhere—

It does not have potential, nor is it dead.
It is a wrecked loom;
do not hang your wash on it.

I am offered tea at every place the paths meet.
The circle of tea is like a locked sun,
or a fish with a tail
so good at being a tail
it reaches its head again
and makes the head a tail,
until it is one round tail.

Tea, tea,
wise as the sea,
tell me how to be with child.
The tea instead offers
a steady stream of limbs.

Buddha says *fire, fire, put out the fire!*
Everything burns here,
but not like Buddha says:
not from a fire-hoop around the head
where the flames point in.

Rather, flames take
the shapes of hammers and nails and lumber
around the burning things.

The new day is slid underneath
the old days:
The clouds can hear only themselves,
the wind can hear only itself,
the old sky grows dark and idiotic, and becomes heaven,
the sun wrenches itself open:

Babylon before Eden,
orchard before garden,
our variety before variety,
shame before shame-knowledge:
When shame was an entity
wandering even from the body
into the tea,
into the brass doves,
into this autobiographical moment.

I must take full responsibility. Quite right. I will move on.

UNIVERSE WHERE WE WEREN'T ARTISTS

I am given a reward:
You two will pick
where I rest.

[handwritten: ceding control]

We are three sweet hunters gazing
at the fat-soaked bog.

[handwritten: power]

Down each gun-hole
we seek the glass lens

that would explode the image
of our prey.

A cuff of air.
We look up to
the hilarious moon.

[handwritten: we/I]

I fall down in white mud.

[handwritten: P 63]

When the breath starts to be ragged,
tickle me, my deepest beloveds—
so that the raggedness becomes confused.

Acknowledgments

This book is dedicated to my family. I hope that art is an act of unconditional love. And my family taught me what unconditional love is. Mom, you love with mythic power—you're my spirit guide, my healer, my larger than life. I have never and will never encounter another human being of such proportions. Your mind, your passions, they barely fit on earth. And of course, it was you (who else could it be?) who gave me the fire, Prometheus—of course it was you who taught me to write. You alone, starting with the alphabet and going up through ten-page short stories with four-syllable words. Victoria, my wife, somewhere, in my time of knowing you, the eye contact changed, and the uncrossable chasm was crossed—you became family. And not just family, but a self for me to be that is better than my wildest imagination. Your love has made me as close to whole as I've ever been, and I do not fear the dark anymore. I think heaven is just an eternity of us telling one another jokes. Dad, you kept my metaphors clear and simple, and kept my mind skeptical but never cynical, and always treated my small emotions with respect, since they were emotions. This is all I think good poetry is. My departed stepfather Alan, you never for a moment stopped demanding my mind and heart rise to the occasion, and you loved me as blindly as blood would've had you. You paved the way for my complete embrace of Victoria, in teaching me that family is chosen. My stepfather Frank, you are my body when my body is too weak, and my spirit when my spirit is too weak. You are very literally carrying my body over this last dark threshold of cancer. You are everything Jesus wanted people to be. My sister Torrie, my other mommy, I never left your hip. Alan taught me family is chosen. You taught me that every family member is all roles to all others when the family is loving enough. And Skye, dear sister so like me, the family's only other artist, the only other to walk so close to death, where would I be without the example of your sweetness and mirth, without watching you, at every turn, use creativity as the antidote to suffering?

There are many people to thank. I have been richer in love and support than anyone I've ever met. I'm sorry if I missed you on this list of thank-yous. It's just a partial roll call of the many ships that sailed to Troy with me.

Milkweed family, you've stunned me. I had no idea a book could get into the world this quickly and this beautiful. In our very short time together, you've exerted yourselves like gods to make this book happen. It matters to you. I matter to you. It couldn't be faked. In a period of life marked by meaninglessness and incalculable loss, you gave me a project, a permanence, a stability, a bit of self-esteem, a bit of joy. Daniel, my general, you moved heaven and earth and always had an extra moment to ask me how my day was. Aoife and Joanna and Joey, you took up the tasks of making this book be beyond my wildest expectations. Martha Collins, dear pressmate and shadchan, thank you for believing in this work without first giving me the chance to charm the crap out of you. I don't think any publisher on this green earth has ever made a rookie writer feel the way you've all made me feel. You've convinced me I'm royalty. I am.

Elizabeth Metzger, dear best friend, dear chosen sister, this book is almost as much yours as mine. Every poem in this book, as soon as a first draft was written, was posted to your inbox. I'd mail at midnight and by morning, your hands were on the poem, your brain and heart were in the poem, it was irrevocably Elizabethed. For reading my mind, and becoming my mind, and extending my mind. For always demanding drama and beauty and brilliance, for piercing me with your insight. I am so grateful. And for holding my hand through more chemos than I can count, I am so grateful. Without Elizabeth, there is no Max.

And Andrew Kahn and Shon Arieh-Lerer, without you there is no Max. For the past four years we've built our minds together. You've taught me that there is no beauty without comedy, and no comedy without beauty. You are my sweet hunters. With my last breaths you will tickle me, so that the raggedness becomes confused. You edited this book, you taught me how to read my work out loud, you slept in my bed when I had scans the next morning. I love you, superheart.

I thank Louise Glück, who gave me my voice. You taught me that I was an artist. You made me the artist I am. Your passion for my work is what allows me to see it. For the countless hours and dozens of drafts you took this book through, I'm so grateful I'm speechless. Your DNA is deep in every page. But while I have so many brilliant notes in your hand in my margins, my very favorite is your signature at the bottom of my wedding certificate.

I thank Sarah Ruhl, my spiritual advisor and this book's dharma guide. You've propped me up with your luminous compassion, and taught me how to be the human I want to be. I promise to reincarnate near you, so that you can keep on teaching me.

I thank Tim Donnelly, my thesis advisor, for being my birthing hospital. Your brilliant mind and eye took a welter of poems and let me see trajectories, root systems, all the implications and complications of who I am and what I am trying to say.

I thank Lucie Brock-Broido, master of my letters, for teaching me how to demand poems, to have my way with them once they had their way with me. Lucie, too, I must thank you for healing my heart with your boundless sensitivity and Herculean patience—I came to Columbia on the verge of giving up on life and left it eager to write and write and write until my life gives out. And it was thanks to the hours you spent teasing me and comforting me that this was so.

I thank Jean Valentine, kooky evil genius of kindness, and the most beautiful laugh I've ever heard in my life. You've lit me on fire with your warmth, with your poems, with your notes on my poems. The moments spent in Holy Communion with you and Elizabeth, Emily Dickinson etched on the wall and croissants on the table, are some of my most sacred memories.

I thank Cynthia Zarin, the Yankee hook who has pulled me out of self-pity and set me back to writing and loving and thinking more times than I can count. Where would I be without you, Cynthia, who got me to read someone other than Berryman? Who made me pay attention to language's texture for the first time? Who has made me pasta, and shared with me Beasie Goddu, your daughter, who has become the smarter-than-me little sister I always wanted?

I thank Dottie Lasky, my thunderbird, for whom I wrote my chapbook, *AEONS*. Dottie, you gave me my first rituals. My whole life is rituals now. My whole life is Dottie. I can't tell you how much our friendship has meant to me. To be there for you, and to have you there for me. We were never strangers. We were always writing poems together. I love you.

Dear Melissa Carroll, my painter. Up there in heaven, I hope you have prepared a living room for us. Riddled with the most baffling knickknacks from every corner of the universe. Whimsical, but tasteful. Beautiful glass bongs on the coffee table with sweet White Widow tamped in the bowls. I hope you've memorized the number of the best Indian restaurant in heaven. And that you've curated an infinite list of bizarre, disorienting comedies on Netflix. Thank you for being a true artist, and for sharing the burden of Ewing's Sarcoma with me. You were my Virgil in all this: the grandest, most bizarre, most disorienting Comedy. I followed. Am following. Keep me safe, I pray.

I thank Alan Ziegler, Big Wig Zig, for being my guidepost to a lifepath full of Buddhist-shtetl humor, deep compassion, and lucid, gorgeous writing. I will never forget your performance of your own work. It changed the way I read and am. And I will never forget the wonderful drinks at Candle 79. And my time spent with your luminous Erin. Victoria and I often say we want to grow up to be you two as a couple.

I thank Sarah Matthes, my poem-kin, writer who shares my project, for her invaluable insight over many years into this book and the many poems that preceded it, and into me as a person. Our love is deep and true, and I can always rely on you to know what my heart is trying to say in a poem, even when the words aren't quite there yet. Every poet needs a reader like that.

I thank Sarah Blake, who has taught me so much and become such a magnificent friend in such a condensed period of time. Your work makes me feel like no one else's in the world does, and your comments on my work make me feel so loved, so understood, and so almost-there-but-here's-exactly-the-right-solution. You make sure I'm safe in this big crazy poetry world, and I couldn't ask for a better big poetry sister in my corner. And you are the best person in the world to text in the middle of the night during a panic attack.

I thank Jenny Franklin and Fred Marchant, the lions who not only put their ink on my work, but pounded every door they could to help this book see light. And thanks to you two, it did! Jenny, you have laser vision and a heart of sugar. And Frank, you are a wise hand parting the waves. I love you, thank you.

Dear Herb Leibowitz, my Parnassus Poppa, the pressure you've put on my words has made me ever more committed to lucidity and to music. I have no patience for trying to make a sentence harder than it should be. The effort goes into making the sentence clear, simple. You taught me that. You and Susan opened your home to me, made me soup when I was down, and generally have been my surrogate family. Thank you, I love you.

I thank Tom Waits for believing in my poems. Tom, you were the first artist I ever took in the complete work of. I found you at age twelve, and by age thirteen I'd heard everything you'd ever released, and could sing *Alice* and *The Black Rider* cover to cover. You shaped my sense of beauty and mystery more than anyone else on the planet has. And I thank Nina Simone for teaching me that I wish I could feel how it is to be free. My time spent with you, Tom and Nina, has given me faith that a human voice can reach right into another's heart.

I thank Brave Stan Possick, shrink of my days and nights. There were many times I almost lost my life to my grief, and your compassion pulled me back. And I thank Abraham Bartel for taking me through the crucible of cancer, and teaching me how to leap to my own defense with psychotherapy, CBT, really whatever it was that could do me right in that particular moment. I thank Herbert Eveloff, my childhood shrink, for making existentialism comprehensible to a hysteric nine-year-old, and for teaching me what a wonderful thing therapy is. I thank Stuart Ende for loving me and my words and caring for my brain in this last little spell of time.

So many people were incredible editors on this book and/or the poems in it. Justin Boening, you wrecked and rocked this book. And thanks to Ava Kofman, Rachel Kauder Nalebuff, Ethan Kuperberg, Suleika Jaouad, Dan Attanasio, Noah Warren, Will Brewer, my beautiful thesis workshop team—especially Hannah Rogers—and Jonathan Galassi, Ngozi Ukazu, Russell Bennetts, Abby Schulman, Carlie Hoffman, Sandy McClatchy, Eliza Schrader, and Kathleen Ossip.

I thank my doctors, who have kept me alive to write this book. Paul Meyers, Melinda Merchant, Michael Laquaglia, Suzanne Wolden, David Schrump, Peter Boasberg, Robert and Kathy McKenna, Charles Forscher, Kumar Sankhala, Sunil Sharma, John Nemunaitis, Jim O'Dorisio, Stephen Lesnick, Gary Kupfer, and Patrick Grohar.

Autumn Von Plinsky, thank you for the phenomenal cover art— our art will always be together now! Fathomless thanks to Mary Austin Speaker, my designer, for her sensitive scouring of every bone in this book and every blemish on its skin. And my extended family who has taken care of me over the years: my "Uncle Needle" Shai Golan and his mishpacha, Rayon Black, Marco Campobosso, Braylan Ritvo, David Jackson-Hanen, Kathryn Jackson, Allen and Anya Hanen, Michele and David Slifka, Chris and Chelsea Dato, Marissa Nestor, William Zabel, Maria Medrano, Sandra Espinola, Flor Medrano, Don and Shana Passman and the Passman Clan, the Schulman Clan, Mark and Debbie Attanasio, Judy and Morris Sarna, Betsy and Alan Cohn, Shira and Jimmy Levin, Gary and Phyllis Gladstein, Andres Martin and the whole Martin Clan, Demetra Hufnagel, Norm and Mary Pattiz, Sam and Marion Waxman, Mark and Harriet Borovitz, Elimelech Goldberg and the Kids Kicking Cancer family, Laila Maher, and the singular, brilliant Penelope Laurans.

***

Boston Review: "Afternoon," "Black Bulls," "Heaven Is Us Being a Flower Together," "Poem About My Wife Being Perfect and Me Being Afraid" (published as "Poem About You Being Perfect and Me Being Afraid"), "Radiation in New Jersey, Convalescence in New York," "The Senses"
Chronogram: "Second Dream" (published as "Tages")
Iowa Review: "Poem Set in the Day and in the Night"
The Journal: "The Blimp"
Lit Hub: "The End"
Los Angeles Review of Books: "Poem to My Dog, Monday, on Night I Accidentally Ate Meat"
The New Yorker: "Poem to My Litter"
Plume: "Mommy Harangues Poor Randal," "To Randal, Crow-Stealer, Lord of the Greenhouse," "The Curve"
POETRY: "Dawn of Man," "The Big Loser"
Poets.org Poem-a-Day: "Touching the Floor"
Poets/Artists: "The Watercolor Eulogy" (published as "To the Hands of My Painter")
Slate: "The Hanging Gardens," "Universe Where We Weren't Artists"
St. Ann's Review: "Sky-Sex Dreams of Randal"
The Yale Review: "Living It Up"

from *AEONS*, 2014 Poetry Society of America Chapbook awarded by Jean Valentine: "Appeal to My First Love" (published as "Where I Laughed"), "Hi, Melissa" (published as "Still"), "The Senses," "Universe Where We Weren't Artists," "Lyric Complicity for One" (published as "Lyric Complicity")

Ashley Woo

MAX RITVO (1990–2016) wrote *Four Reincarnations* in New York and Los Angeles over the course of a long battle with cancer. He was also the author of the chapbook *AEONS*, chosen by Jean Valentine to receive the Poetry Society of America Chapbook Fellowship in 2014. Ritvo's poetry has appeared in the *New Yorker*, *Poetry*, and the *Boston Review*, and as a Poem-a-Day for Poets.org. His prose and interviews have appeared in publications such as Lit Hub, *Huffington Post*, and the *Los Angeles Review of Books*.

Interior design & typesetting by Mary Austin Speaker
Typeset in Fournier

Fournier is a typeface created by the Monotype Corporation in 1924, based on types cut in the mid-eighteenth century by Pierre-Simon Fournier, a French typographer. The specific cuts used as a reference for Fournier are referred to as "St Augustin Ordinaire" in Fournier's influential *Manuel Typographique*, published in 1764 in Paris.